MODERN FOLK EMBROIDERY

MODERN FOLK EMBROIDERY

NANCY NICHOLSON

D&C

David and Charles

www.sewandso.co.uk

CONTENTS

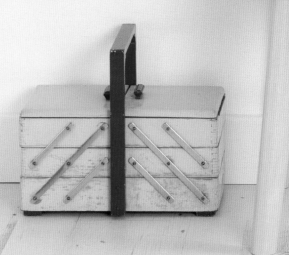

INTRODUCTION

The urge to embellish and decorate the objects around us seems to be fundamental to who we are: it's evident even in the earliest traces of humankind. Every culture has its own distinctive way with design. Colour and stitch are very much part of this, apparent everywhere in decorative pattern, from national costumes to home interiors.

I grew up with a heightened awareness of design, particularly textile design. My father Roger Nicholson was a professor of fine art textiles at the Royal College of Art. My mother Joan was a pioneering force in the Needlework Development Scheme of the 1960s and '70s, teaching and writing on new ways with stitch. She was heavily influenced by folk art from across the world, particularly Scandinavia and China. These were my own earliest, strongest influences as I watched her working at home and absorbed her love of decoration.

My mother believed that embroidery could be enjoyed by all and was determined to spread the word. She died a few years ago but would have been thrilled to see the resurgent interest in craft as we've come to appreciate again the simple soothing pleasures of working steadily with our hands in thread and fabric.

It was in my mother's spirit of innovation, combined with the inspiration of folk culture, that I started to produce my own range of embroidery kits, and I have now written this book to share my designs with you.

TOOLS AND MATERIALS

Listed here are all the tools and materials you will need to complete the projects. If you are a keen stitcher, you may already have most of these to hand, but I hope this serves as a useful checklist. You'll also need access to a sewing machine for making up many of the projects.

NEEDLES

While it is always good to have a variety of needles in your sewing box, I have used only two types of needle for the project embroideries: a tapestry needle with a blunt end and wide eye, size 22, and crewel embroidery needles, sizes 3 and 5.

STRANDED EMBROIDERY COTTON (FLOSS)

This is thread made of six strands and these can be pulled apart to the required thickness. In general, I have used three strands for the project embroideries. Be sure to buy a quality brand such as Anchor or DMC. You'll find that it comes in a huge range of colours.

TAPESTRY WOOL (YARN)

I use Anchor or Appletons tapestry wool (yarn) in either 2-ply or 4-ply, although you could use leftover yarn from your knitting stash. You'll need to use a tapestry needle when embroidering with yarn.

SCISSORS

You'll need a collection of good-quality scissors: a pair of general purpose scissors for cutting card templates; a pair of dedicated fabric cutting scissors; and sharp embroidery scissors for snipping your threads. I use a pinking cutting wheel to cut the zigzag edge on felts, but you could use pinking shears if you prefer.

FABRICS

You can embroider on just about anything, so take a look at what you have to hand and experiment. For the embroideries onto felt, I have used a 'heathered' felt that has a marled effect, so the colours are much more subtle than with nylon felts (see Suppliers). For the embroideries onto fabric, I've mostly used linen, which can be stabilized for embroidery by applying an iron-on interfacing. For the tote bag I chose hardwearing ticking fabric, which is great to embroider onto as the lines are easy to follow when stitching. For bag linings, choose lightweight cotton.

TRANSFER TOOLS

- Air-erasable pen
- Iron-on transfer pen
- Pencils and tracing paper
- Thin card for making templates

EMBROIDERY HOOP

It is a matter of personal choice whether you use a hoop for keeping your fabric taut as you embroidery – I prefer to simply hold my embroidery in my hand.

OTHER ESSENTIALS

- Pins
- Polyester stuffing
- Machine sewing cotton in project appropriate colours
- Brooch backs
- Self-cover buttons
- Decorative buttons
- Cotton tapes in project appropriate colours
- Black elastic cord (rounded)
- Tape measure
- Craft foam 2–3mm (approx. 1/8in) thick

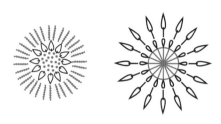   

STITCH LIBRARY

If you are a beginner you will soon come to know what experienced embroiderers understand, that embroidery is a relaxing and mindful craft. It is so easy to get started with even just a few basic stitches. Just choose your project, transfer your design (for methods, see Techniques), thread your needle, make a knot at the end of your thread and get stitching.

Over the next few pages I am going to show you to how to work the stitches used for the projects and motifs featured in this book, plus a few more for you to discover as you develop your embroidery skills. These stitches have been organized into colour-coded families. Accompanying each project, I have provided you with embroidery suggestions to guide you as you stitch and these show the stitches I have used, but as you become more confident you can substitute these with your own choice of stitches.

Throughout the book there are pages of stitch combinations for you to explore, offering you exciting opportunities to combine stitches in a variety of ways to create very different effects. It is my hope that you will be inspired to work rich and varied combinations of your own.

● RUNNING STITCH FAMILY

Running stitch can look wonderful worked on its own to define the hem of a pinafore dress or the edge of a sampler picture, but it is also the start point for so many exciting embroidery stitches. The basic stitch can be decorated in so many ways, whipped and laced to great effect.

Running Stitch

Back Stitch

Whipped Running Stitch

STITCH LIBRARY

Laced Running Stitch

Double Laced Running Stitch

Eskimo Laced Running Stitch

Parallel Laced Running Stitch

Stepped Running Stitch

Stepped Running Stitch Variation

Couching Stitch

● HERRINGBONE STITCH FAMILY

Herringbone stitch is a quick, easy stitch to work, but it can be developed in so many different ways. You can lace it to give it a braided effect, or doubled up in a contrasting colour, and it can easily be combined with other stitches – try working running stitch over the overlapping crosses or simple cross stitch in between the diagonals.

Herringbone Stitch

Double Herringbone Stitch

Laced Herringbone Stitch

Tacked Herringbone Stitch and Variations

● CHAIN STITCH FAMILY

Chain stitch is a firm favourite as it has so many simple variations once the basic method has been learnt. It is a useful filler stitch, and worked as a detached stitch it makes lovely flower petals and stylized leaf shapes. It can also be laced, or emboldened with running stitch.

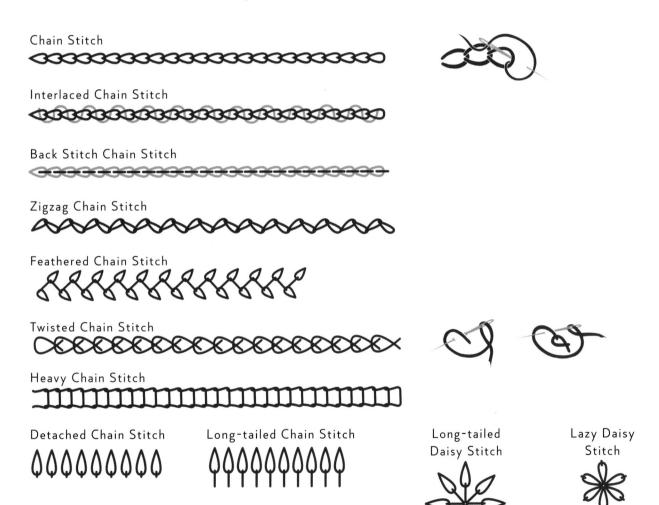

Chain Stitch

Interlaced Chain Stitch

Back Stitch Chain Stitch

Zigzag Chain Stitch

Feathered Chain Stitch

Twisted Chain Stitch

Heavy Chain Stitch

Detached Chain Stitch

Long-tailed Chain Stitch

Long-tailed Daisy Stitch

Lazy Daisy Stitch

● BUTTONHOLE STITCH FAMILY

Buttonhole stitch is often used as an edging stitch on embroidery, but it really comes into its own to create circular shapes. It can also be used to create loops for fixings and buttons.

Buttonhole Stitch

Double Buttonhole Stitch

Buttonhole Wheel Stitch

Buttonhole Flower Stitch

  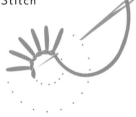

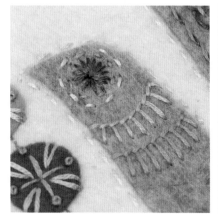

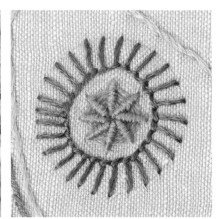

STITCH LIBRARY

● FLY AND FEATHER STITCH FAMILY

Fly stitch is a great favourite of mine and detached fly stitch frequently pops up in my embroidery. Worked as a line, fly stitch can be whipped with a contrasting thread for added decoration. Fly stitch and the little more challenging feather stitch make great flower stems, especially when tipped with detached chain stitch or French knots.

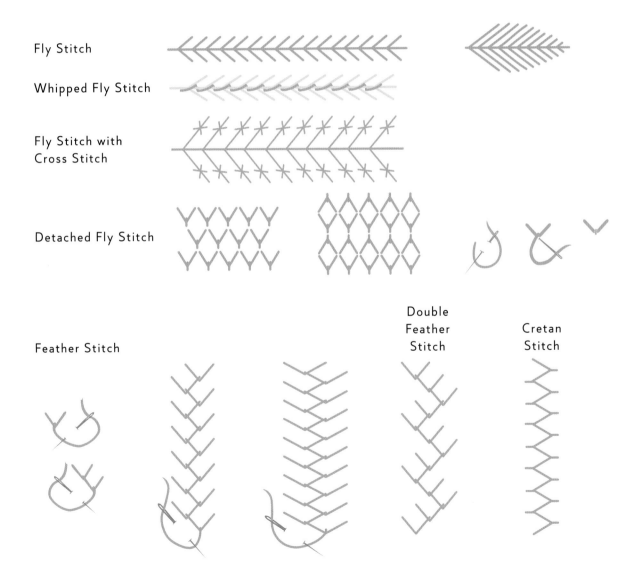

Fly Stitch

Whipped Fly Stitch

Fly Stitch with
Cross Stitch

Detached Fly Stitch

Feather Stitch

Double
Feather
Stitch

Cretan
Stitch

● SPOT STITCH FAMILY

Many stitches can be used to create focal points in a design, such as a spider's web flower centre, star stitch highlights, decorative shapes made from simple straight stitch, or a satin stitch filling, for eyes for example.

Star Stitch

Small Star
Stitch Variation

Double Star Stitch

Cross Stitch

Long-tailed
Cross Stitch

Spider's Web Stitch

Satin Stitch

Straight Stitch

● KNOT STITCH FAMILY

Knot stitches are a wonderful way to add texture to your embroidery as they give a lovely beaded effect to your work. Once mastered, they make a great addition to your repertoire of stitches, so spend some time practising them until you get even knots every time.

French Knots

Bullion Knot Stitch

Coral Knot Stitch

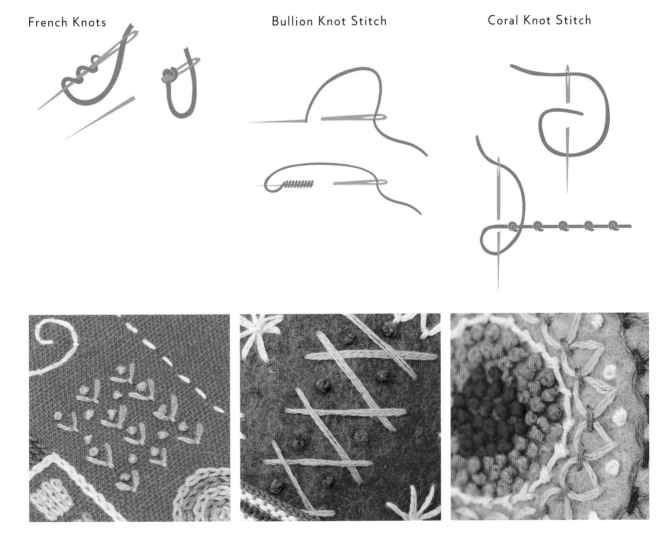

THE PROJECTS

Whether you're a beginner or a more experienced embroiderer, you'll find plenty in these pages to inspire you. This is a practical book designed to help you make some lovely things, and I've applied traditional stitching techniques to fresh designs, at the same time drawing ideas from different cultures. The projects should prove satisfying in themselves but I hope they'll also give you the confidence to take these ideas and skills in other directions, following your own tastes and sources of inspiration, and that this is just the beginning of your creative journey.

PINCUSHIONS

Here are two easy pincushions for you to choose from. Quick and simple to make, each provides you with endless opportunities to practise new stitches. Discover how to cover a simple form with felt to make the bottle-cap pincushion, and keep your sewing needles handy with the secret needle keeper in the rectangular pincushion.

- -

YOU WILL NEED

Felt in a choice of colours

Polyester stuffing

Stranded embroidery cotton (floss) in a choice of colours

Double-sided tape and a wine-bottle cap for the bottle-cap pincushion

Large press-stud for the rectangular pincushion

BOTTLE-CAP PINCUSHION

MAKING UP

1. Trace the bottle-cap pincushion templates (see Templates) onto thin card and cut out.

2. Use a pencil to draw around the card templates onto your chosen felt colours and cut out your pieces (one side, one base, one top).

3. Put a small square of double-sided tape on both the side and the base of the bottle cap to hold the felt in place as you sew.

4. Cover the side of the cap with the long felt strip and the base with the small felt circle. Over-sew around the base and up the side.

5. Take the large felt circle and sew a line of gathering (long running) stitches 3mm (⅛in) from the edge.

6. Place a small ball of stuffing (about the size of an egg when squeezed) into the centre and draw up the thread to close tight. Stitch to hold.

7. Push the padded top firmly into the cap and slip stitch all the way around to attach it to the bottle-cap base.

8. Now embroider using three strands of the embroidery thread and your own choice of stitches or refer to Embroidery Suggestions for inspiration.

At a glance

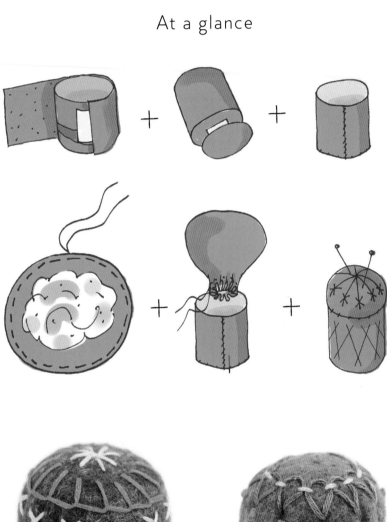

EMBROIDERY SUGGESTIONS

Embroider your design using the stitch suggestions displayed here. Refer to the Stitch Library for instructions for working the embroidery stitches.

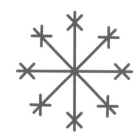

- ● Eskimo Laced Running Stitch
- ● Laced Herringbone Stitch, Tacked Herringbone Stitch
- ● Whipped Fly Stitch, Detached Fly Stitch
- ● Double Star Stitch, Cross Stitch, Long-tailed Cross Stitch

RECTANGULAR PINCUSHION

MAKING UP

1. Use the rectangular pincushion templates (see Templates) to cut out the felt pieces for the large (with needle keeper) or small rectangular pincushion.

2. Embroider the pincushion top using three strands of the embroidery thread (see Embroidery Suggestions), taking care not to go over the seam allowance.

3. If making a needle keeper, stitch the insert onto the back of the needle keeper flap.

4. Pink the edges of the flap, or embroider with buttonhole stitch if you prefer. Tack (baste) the needle keeper in place on the front of the pincushion.

5. Place the back and front together with right sides facing and machine stitch all around the edge using a 1cm (½in) seam allowance and leaving a 6cm (2½in) opening.

6. Trim the corners and turn right side out, pushing out the corners carefully to a point.

7. Fill with stuffing, then turn in the seam allowance on the opening and sew it closed by hand as neatly as you can.

8. Use the button templates to cut out two circles of felt and one of craft foam. Embroider one felt circle (see Embroidery Suggestions).

9. Place the foam circle in between the felt circles and buttonhole stitch together. Sew the finished button to the top or side.

10. To complete the needle keeper, remove tacking (basting) stitches and stitch a press-stud to the underside of the flap to secure it in place when not in use (the button embellishment should be positioned to hide the stitching).

At a glance

EMBROIDERY SUGGESTIONS

Embroider your design using the stitch suggestions displayed here. Refer to the Stitch Instructions section for illustration of the different embroidery stitches.

- ● Eskimo Laced Running Stitch
- ● Detached Chain Stitch
- ● Buttonhole Stitch
- ● Fly Stitch, Detached Fly Stitch, Feather Stitch
- ● Star Stitch, Straight Stitch
- ● French Knots

CUFF BRACELET

This pretty little cuff bracelet is a very traditional Scandinavian accessory, and it will help to keep your wrists warm as you embroider your way through cold, winter days. It is so simple to make and only takes a few strips of felt and a little embroidery to create something very special.

YOU WILL NEED

6.5cm x 20cm (2½in x 8in) cream felt

5.5cm x 20cm (2¼in x 8in) red felt (pinked)

4.5cm x 20cm (1¾in x 8in) pink felt (pinked)

2cm x 20cm (¾in x 8in) green felt (pinked)

Two pearl buttons

Stranded embroidery cotton (floss) in a choice of colours

Black elastic cord

MAKING UP

1. The measurements given are for my wrist size. Measure your wrist and add a little extra for ease. Adjusting the sizes as necessary, cut all the pieces of felt, pinking the red, pink and green strips only down the long edges.

2. Layer the pinked felt strips, centring them as you go, and tack (baste) to hold in place.

3. Embroider the design using three strands of the embroidery thread (see Embroidery Suggestions) working your stitches over the strips of felt to hold them together. Remove tacking (basting) stitches.

4. Cut a piece of elastic 10cm (4in) long and knot the ends together to make a loop big enough to go over your buttons. Make one more button loop and stitch them in place along the short end of the remaining cream felt strip.

5. Place the cream strip over the back of the embroidered panel and attach together with running stitch.

6. Sew on the buttons to align with the button loops at the opposite end of the cuff bracelet.

At a glance

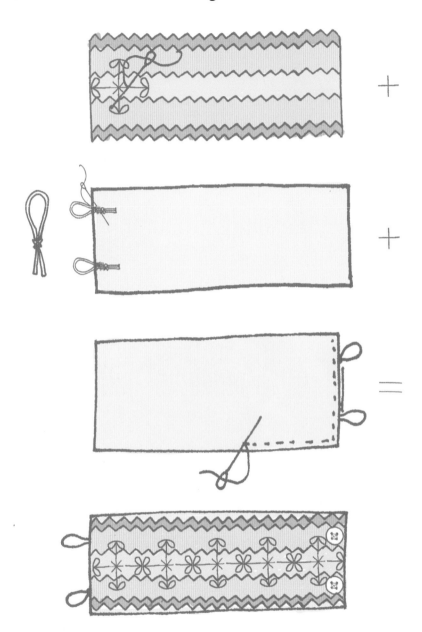

CUFF BRACELET

EMBROIDERY SUGGESTIONS

Embroider your design using the stitch suggestions displayed here. Refer to the Stitch Library for instructions for working the embroidery stitches.

● Eskimo Laced Running Stitch

● Long-tailed Chain Stitch

● Spider's Web Stitch, Star Stitch

GEOMETRIC GARLAND

These decorations are made from shapes cut out of felt and embroidered, then stiffened by sandwiching craft foam in between. There are templates for making the circles in three different sizes and the diamonds are made extra colourful by adding a smaller diamond appliqué to the centre. They don't take long and can be strung together for a festive garland or celebratory streamer, or hung individually.

- -

YOU WILL NEED

Felt in a choice of colours

Stranded embroidery cotton (floss) in a choice of colours

Craft foam

Seed beads (optional)

Decorative cotton tape

MAKING UP

1. Trace the diamond and circle templates (see Templates) onto thin card and cut out, carefully marking which are to be cut from foam and which from felt.

2. Use a pencil to draw around the relevant card templates onto foam and cut out, and mark and cut out the shapes from your chosen felt colours.

3. Embroider the designs using three strands of the embroidery thread (see Embroidery Suggestions) or make up your own combinations of stitches.

4. Sandwich a foam shape in between two felt shapes and slip stitch all around the edge. If using as individual decorations, fold a 6cm (2½in) length of tape in half and incorporate it into the seam to make a hanging loop.

5. For extra sparkle, sew seed beads around the edge of the decorations.

6. To make a garland, use a long needle to sew through the felt to join the decorations onto a length of decorative cotton tape, spacing them evenly.

At a glance

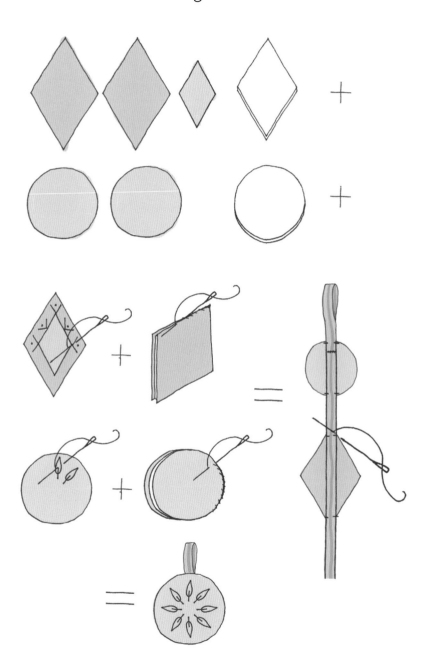

GEOMETRIC GARLAND

EMBROIDERY SUGGESTIONS

Embroider your design using the stitch suggestions displayed here. Refer to the Stitch Library for instructions for working the embroidery stitches.

● Running Stitch, Eskimo Laced Running Stitch, Double Laced Running Stitch

● Chain Stitch, Detached Chain Stitch, Long-tailed Chain Stitch, Lazy Daisy Stitch

● Buttonhole Wheel Stitch, Buttonhole Flower Stitch

● Detached Fly Stitch

● Spider's Web Stitch, Star Stitch, Long-tailed Cross Stitch, Straight Stitch

● French Knots

THREAD
CATCHER

The thread catcher is a little bin to put your cut ends in as you sew, rather than dropping them all over the floor, or the dog! It has a lid that closes with a buttonhole loop to keep threads contained, preventing them from blocking up your vacuum cleaner. Made from red and blue felt with contrasting embroidery, the lid is lightly stuffed to double up as a temporary pincushion.

YOU WILL NEED

Felt in a choice of colours

Polyester stuffing

Stranded embroidery cotton (floss) in a choice of colours

Craft foam

Button

MAKING UP

1. Trace the thread catcher lid and base templates (see Templates) onto thin card and cut out, carefully marking which are to be cut from foam and which from felt. Use the templates to cut out the foam for the lid and base, and the felt for the lid top, lid base and base.

2. Cut the pieces for the pot sides: two strips of felt 5.5cm x 23.5cm (2¼in x 9¼in), and one piece of foam 5cm x 23cm (2in x 9in).

3. To assemble the base and side, sandwich the foam piece in between the two felt pieces and stitch all around using a slip stitch.

4. To make the lid, sandwich the foam in between the lid top and lid base felt pieces. Over-sew a little way around, then place some stuffing in between the foam and the top layer of felt; continue to stitch all the way around easing in to fit.

5. Join the short ends of the side together and over-sew, then attach the base of the pot in the same way.

6. Embroider the side of the pot and the top of the lid using three strands of the embroidery thread (see Embroidery Suggestions).

7. Make a buttonhole loop (see Techniques) at one side of the lid, and attach the lid to the pot with a small rectangle of felt sewn over the pot's inside seam and onto the base of the lid to create a hinge.

8. Attach the button to the pot to align with the buttonhole loop when the lid is closed.

At a glance

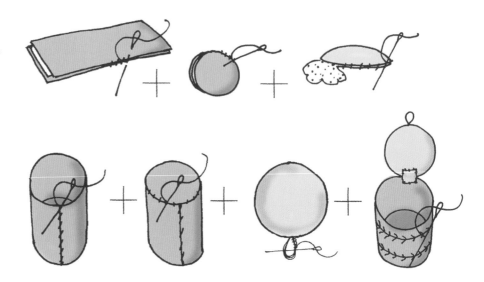

THREAD CATCHER

EMBROIDERY SUGGESTIONS

Embroider your design using the stitch suggestions displayed here. Refer to the Stitch Library for instructions for working the embroidery stitches.

- ● Eskimo Laced Running Stitch
- ● Tacked Herringbone Stitch
- ● Fly Stitch, Feather Stitch
- ● Cross Stitch

Note: Repeat this embroidery design all the way around the side of the pot.

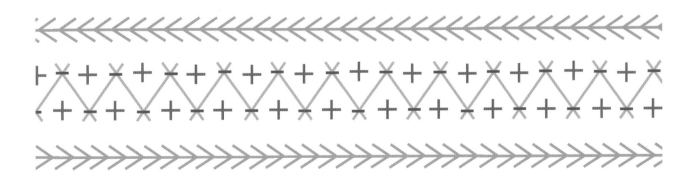

TOTE BAG

This useful tote bag is made from hardwearing ticking and denim fabric, lined with a bright contrasting colour to brighten up a market-shopping trip. Ticking fabric is great to embroider onto if you are a beginner as the fine stripes provide a guide to keep your lines of stitching straight.

- -

YOU WILL NEED

Two pieces of ticking fabric 21.5cm x 33cm (8½in x 13in)

Two pieces of denim or chambray fabric 21.5cm x 33cm (8½in x 13in)

Two strips of denim or chambray fabric 6cm x 54cm (8½in x 21½in)

Two pieces of lining fabric 33cm x 41.5cm (13in x 16¼in)

Stranded embroidery cotton (floss) in a choice of colours

MAKING UP

1. Using the fine stripes as a guide, embroider lines of fly, feather and running stitch using three strands of the embroidery thread (see Embroidery Suggestions) onto one piece of the ticking fabric.

2. With right sides facing, machine stitch the denim pieces to the ticking pieces with a 1.5cm (⅝in) seam allowance to make bag front and back, and press the seams flat.

3. Now embroider the motifs onto the denim piece on the bag front (see Embroidery Suggestions).

4. With right sides facing, machine stitch the bag front to the bag back leaving the top open. Trim corners and turn the bag right side out.

5. Machine stitch the lining pieces together; do not turn right side out.

6. Fold and press a hem all around the top of the lining and the bag. Place the lining inside the bag and tack (baste) in place at the top.

7. Machine stitch around the top edge; finish with hand running stitch.

8. Make handles from the denim strips and attach to the bag.

At a glance

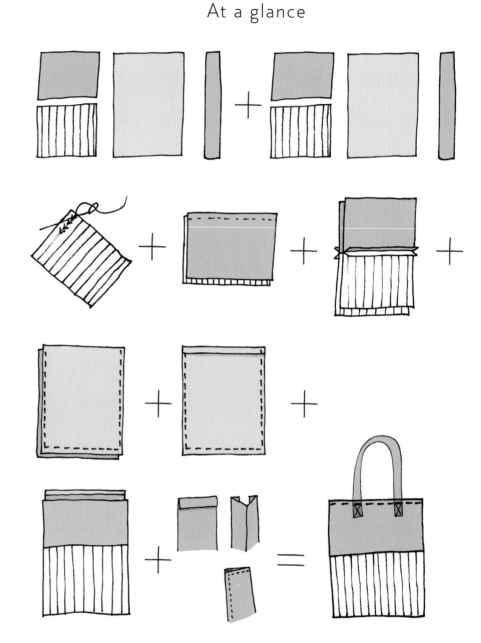

TOTE BAG

EMBROIDERY SUGGESTIONS

Embroider your design using the stitch suggestions displayed here. Refer to the Stitch Library for instructions for working the embroidery stitches.

- ● Running Stitch
- ● Detached Chain Stitch
- ● Feather Stitch, Fly Stitch, Detached Fly Stitch
- ● Star Stitch, Straight Stitch

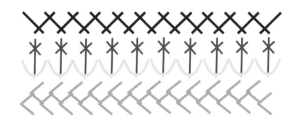

BRAID CUSHION

This cushion is named for the embroidered felt braid that runs across the centre of this colourful accessory. The braid is made separately to the cushion, which is made from boiled wool. Once it is sewn in place, more embroidery is worked to extend the decoration onto the cushion.

- -

YOU WILL NEED

Two strips of felt at least 34cm (13¼in) long

Two pieces of heavyweight woollen fabric 18.5cm x 34cm
(7¼in x 13¼in) in two different colours for front

Two pieces of heavyweight woollen fabric 21.5cm x 34cm
(8½in x 13¼in) in two different colours for back

Large self-cover button

2-ply tapestry wool (yarn) in a choice of colours

30cm (12in) square cushion pad

MAKING UP

1. Using either a pinking cutting wheel or pinking shears, cut one wider length of felt and another narrower one for the braid decoration.

2. Centre the narrow pinked strip on top of the wider pinked strip and tack (baste) together.

3. Using 2-ply tapestry wool (yarn), embroider the three centre lines (see Embroidery Suggestions).

4. Take the woollen fabric pieces for the cushion front and machine stitch them together with a 1.5cm (⅝in) seam allowance.

5. Tack (baste) the embroidered braid to the centre seam of the cushion front.

6. Embroider the detached fly stitch over the outer pinked edges of the felt braid, then the long-tailed cross stitch and finally the rows of herringbone onto the woollen fabric.

7. Carefully remove the tacking (basting) stitches.

8. To make the cushion back, first stitch a double hem on one long edge of the remaining woollen fabric pieces: turn over by 1.5cm (⅝in) and then by the same amount again.

9. Machine a buttonhole in the centre of the hemmed edge of one of the pieces.

10. Use an offcut of felt to cover the self-cover button (see Techniques). Embroider the button (see Embroidery Suggestions), then attach it to the centre of the remaining back piece.

11. Put the button through the buttonhole and pin the back pieces together at the sides.

12. With right sides facing, pin and tack (baste) the front and back pieces together, and machine stitch all around.

13. Trim corners for a neat finish, then turn the cushion right side out, carefully pushing out the corners to a point. Unbutton at the back and insert the cushion pad.

BRAID CUSHION

At a glance

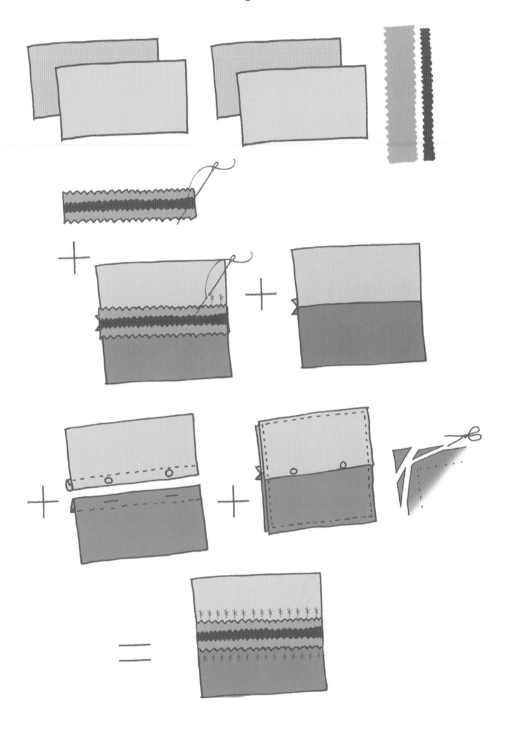

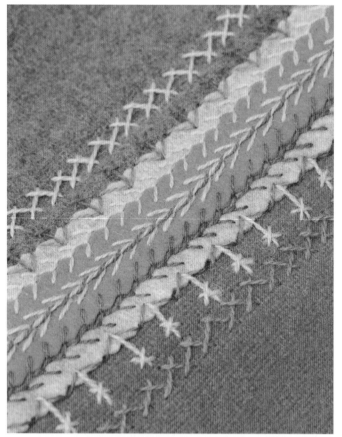

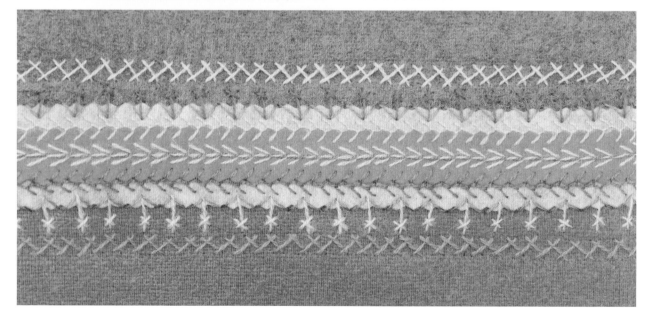

BRAID CUSHION

EMBROIDERY SUGGESTIONS

Embroider your design using the stitch suggestions displayed
here. Refer to the Stitch Library for instructions for working the
embroidery stitches.

- Herringbone Stitch
- Detached Fly Stitch, Whipped Fly Stitch, Feather Stitch
- Long-tailed Cross Stitch

BROOCHES

These flower brooches make lovely gifts. You can make them oval or round, large or small, and choose any colour combination you like. Covering craft foam with felt to make a flower centre, and placing this flower centre on a scalloped petal base, achieves a three-dimensional effect. Add an embroidered leaf for the perfect finishing touch.

- -

YOU WILL NEED

Felt in a choice of colours

Stranded embroidery cotton (floss) in a choice of colours

Craft foam

Brooch backs

MAKING UP

1. Decide which brooch to make and trace the required templates (see Templates) onto thin card and cut out.

2. Use a pencil to draw around the card templates onto the craft foam and your chosen felt colours, and cut out.

3. Embroider your design using three strands of embroidery thread (see Embroidery Suggestions) onto the larger (non-scalloped) piece of felt.

4. Run a line of gathering (long running) stitches around the embroidered piece 3mm (⅛in) from the edge.

5. Place the larger piece of foam on the back of the embroidered piece and draw up the gathering thread making sure that the embroidery is centred. Hold in place with over-sew stitch and knot.

6. Insert the smaller piece of foam to build up depth.

7. Place the petal felt piece on the back of the brooch and stitch all around the edge at the base of each petal using embroidery thread either in the same or a contrasting shade.

8. Sew a brooch back onto the reverse of the petal piece.

9. Add a leaf, if you wish, using the template provided.

At a glance

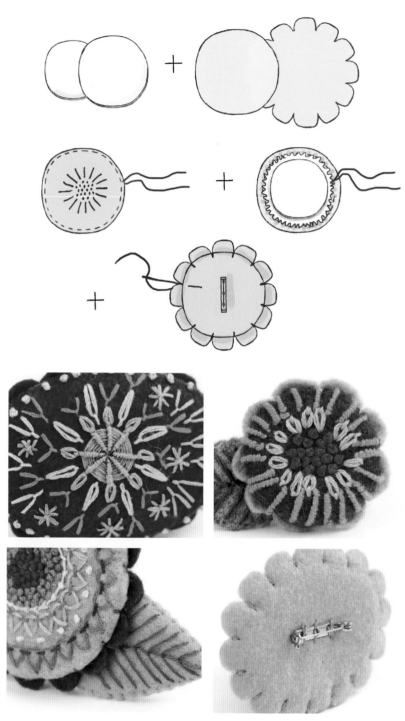

EMBROIDERY SUGGESTIONS

Embroider your design using the stitch suggestions displayed here. Refer to the Stitch Library for instructions for working the embroidery stitches.

- Eskimo Laced Running Stitch
- Detached Chain Stitch, Long-tailed Chain Stitch
- Fly Stitch, Detached Fly Stitch
- Spider's Web Stitch, Star Stitch
- French Knots, Bullion Knot Stitch, Coral Knot Stitch

TABLE RUNNER

This linen table runner will look spectacular on any celebratory table. It is inspired by Scandinavian embroidery, which is always bright and festive. Simply apply the design to the fabric using an iron-on transfer pen ready to work the embroidery. The table runner can easily be extended to suit the length of your table.

YOU WILL NEED

Two pieces of red linen 14cm x 32cm (5½in x 12¾in)

Two pieces of pink linen 20cm x 32cm (8in x 12¾in)

One piece of pale blue linen 32cm x 72cm (12¾in x 28¼in)

One piece of backing fabric of your choice 32cm x 132cm (12¾in x 52in)

Stranded embroidery cotton (floss) in a choice of colours

MAKING UP

1. Machine stitch the red linen pieces to the pink linen pieces using a 1.5cm (⅝in) seam allowance to make the table runner ends.

2. Transfer the embroidery design (see Embroidery Suggestions) to your fabric pieces (see Techniques for options). Take care to space out the motifs correctly.

3. Embroider the designs on all the sections using four strands of the embroidery thread.

4. Stitch together the table runner centre to the two end pieces using a 1.5cm (⅝in) seam allowance.

5. Pin and tack (baste) the backing to the front embroidered panel with right sides facing.

6. Machine stitch all around the panel using a 1cm (½in) seam allowance and leaving a 15cm (6in) opening on the centre panel for turning through.

7. Trim the corners and seams and turn right side out, carefully pushing out the corners to a nice sharp point.

8. Turn in the seam allowance on the opening and hand stitch it closed as neatly as you can. Press to finish.

At a glance

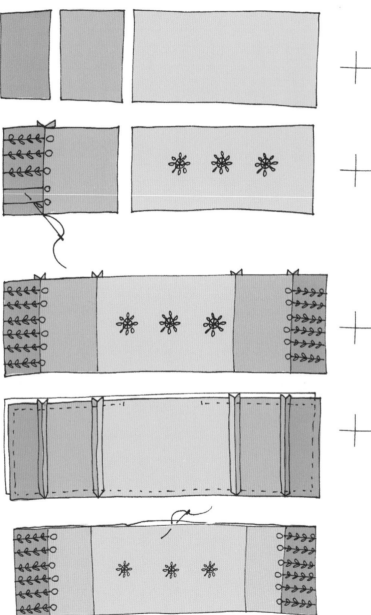

EMBROIDERY SUGGESTIONS

Embroider your design using the stitch suggestions displayed here. Refer to the Stitch Library for instructions for working the embroidery stitches.

- Whipped Running Stitch
- Detached Chain Stitch, Long-tailed Chain Stitch
- Buttonhole Wheel Stitch
- Double Star Stitch
- French Knots

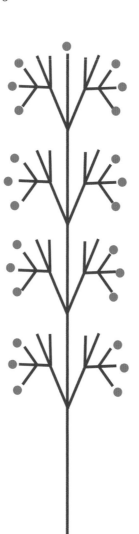

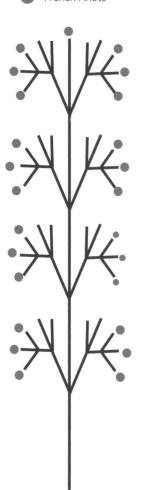

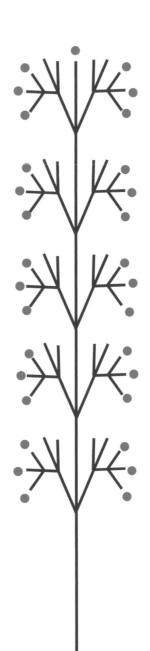

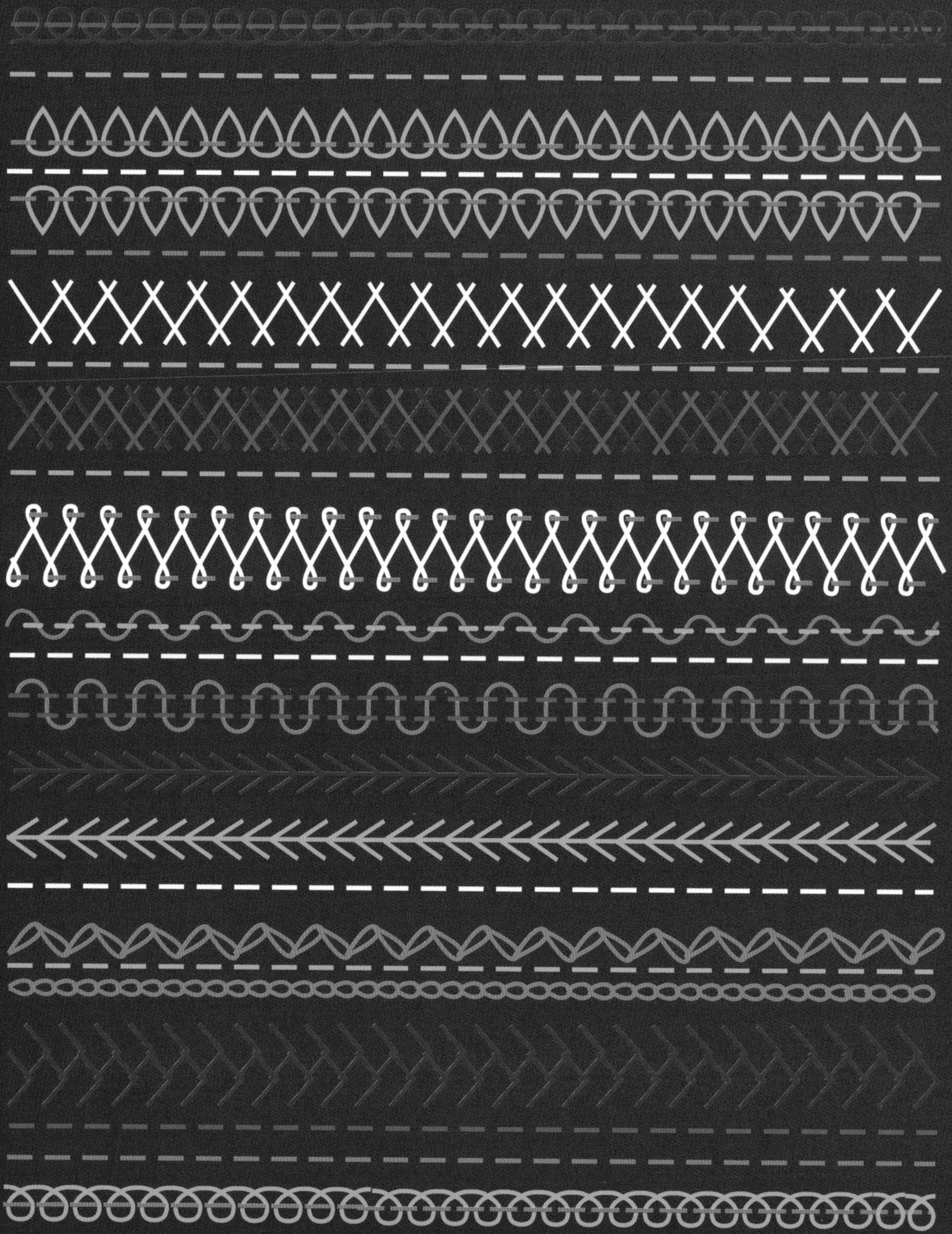

PINAFORE DRESS

This little girl's folk-style pinafore is made from a deep red linen fabric with a contrasting pink pocket. The butterflies and flower embroidery design make this simple dress very special. Although I made the dress, I could just as easily have embroidered the designs, or any of the designs in this book, onto ready-made, shop-bought garments.

- -

YOU WILL NEED

Burda Children's Easy Sewing Pattern No. 9420 Summer
Dress or similar pinafore pattern

Red linen for making dress according to chosen pattern

Small square of pink linen for pocket

Stranded embroidery cotton (floss) in a choice of colours

MAKING UP

1. Cut out and make up the pinafore dress according to the pattern.

2. Transfer the butterfly motifs (see Embroidery Suggestions) to the dress using an iron-on transfer pen (see Techniques).

3. Embroider the designs using three strands of the embroidery thread.

4. Embroider lines of running stitch around the hem, sleeve openings and neckline. (I used pink and white embroidery thread.)

5. Transfer the flower motif to the centre of the pink linen square and embroider the design as before.

6. Turn a small hem along each side of the pocket, then machine stitch it onto the dress.

7. Complete the flower embroidery by working the stem design following the Embroidery Suggestions.

8. Press the dress and the pocket with a damp cloth to finish.

EMBROIDERY SUGGESTIONS

Embroider your design using the stitch suggestions displayed here. Refer to the Stitch Library for instructions for working the embroidery stitches.

- Running Stitch, Back Stitch, Whipped Running Stitch*
- Chain Stitch
- Buttonhole Wheel Stitch
- Fly Stitch, Detached Fly Stitch
- Cross Stitch
- French Knots

Note: These line stitches are relatively interchangeable depending on your preferences. I've generally used whipped running stitch to outline the butterfly wings and back stitch for the butterfly antennae.

CIRCLES CUSHION

The circles motif on this simple-to-make cushion is embroidered on four separate squares before the project is put together, making it very manageable to work. The same design is stitched each time in different colour variations to great effect, and oddments of knitting or tapestry wool (yarn) are used for the easy stitches.

YOU WILL NEED

Four squares of open weave heavyweight linen 21cm
(8¼in) square in colour of your choosing

Two rectangles of backing fabric 24cm x 39cm
(9½in x 15¼in)

Oddments of knitting or tapestry wool (yarn)

Two self-cover buttons

35.5cm (14in) square cushion pad

MAKING UP

1. Machine zigzag all around each linen square to prevent the fabric fraying as you embroider.

2. Print out or trace off the circles template (see Templates) and transfer it to the centre of each linen square using an iron-on transfer or air-erasable pen (see Techniques).

3. Embroider the design using tapestry wool (yarn) changing the colours used for each square (see Embroidery Suggestions).

4. Machine stitch the squares together using a 1.5cm (⅝in) seam allowance and press the seams open.

5. To make the cushion back, first stitch a double hem on one long edge of the two rectangles of backing fabric: turn over by 1.5cm (⅝in) and then by the same amount again.

6. Machine buttonholes at either end of the hemmed edge of one of the backing pieces.

7. Cover the buttons (see Techniques) and embroider with motifs of your choosing. Attach the buttons to the remaining back piece and put the buttons through the buttonholes. Pin the back pieces together at the sides.

8. With right sides facing, pin and tack (baste) the front and back together, and machine stitch all around. Trim corners for a neat finish, then turn the cushion right side out, carefully pushing out the corners to a point. Unbutton at the back and insert the cushion pad.

At a glance

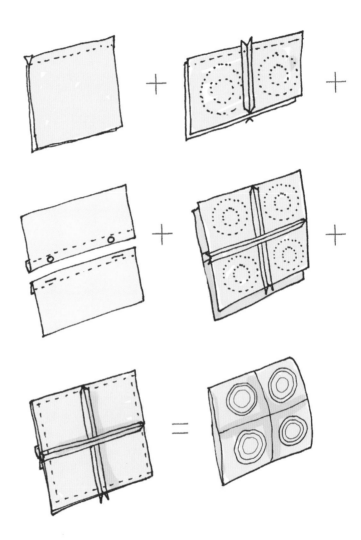

EMBROIDERY SUGGESTIONS

Embroider your design using the stitch suggestions displayed here. Refer to the Stitch Library for instructions for working the embroidery stitches.

- ● Eskimo Laced Running Stitch, Running Stitch
- ● Herringbone Stitch
- ● Chain Stitch, Long-tailed Chain Stitch
- ● Detached Fly Stitch
- ● Straight Stitch for centre grid: use a small diagonal stitch to anchor at each crossover point.

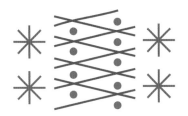

FOLK DOLL

This little doll, stitched completely from felt, is just the right size to fit little hands. Her dress is incorporated into the body pattern while embroidery creates the bodice and apron detailing. Her bunches are made from scraps of yarn and are so easy to style.

YOU WILL NEED

Felt in a choice of colours
(I used cream for the doll and pink for the dress)

Cotton sewing thread to match felt colours

Polyester stuffing

Stranded embroidery cotton (floss) in a choice of colours

Knitting wool (yarn)

Narrow ribbon approximately 60cm (24in) long

MAKING UP

1. Trace the doll templates (see Templates) onto thin card or paper and cut out.

2. Use the templates to cut out all the pieces of the doll (two heads, two bodies, four arms, four legs) in your chosen felt colours.

3. Using a matching cotton sewing thread, over-sew the pieces together leaving an opening at the top of the limbs, the top of the body and the base of the head for stuffing.

4. Stuff the head and body well, then over-sew the head to the body.

5. Stuff the limbs and stitch the openings closed.

6. Embroider the face, the dress and the limbs using three strands of the embroidery thread (see Embroidery Suggestions). For the arms and legs, continue the embroidery all the way around to the back of the limbs.

7. Hand stitch the doll's arms and legs to the body.

8. To make the hair, cut 20 lengths of wool (yarn) each measuring about 15cm (6in) long and place on the top seam of the head.

9. Over-sew each strand, gather into bunches and slip stitch to the side of the neck. Tie a 15cm (6in) length of ribbon around each bunch.

10. Use the remaining ribbon for the dress waistband, tying it into a bow at the back.

FOLK DOLL

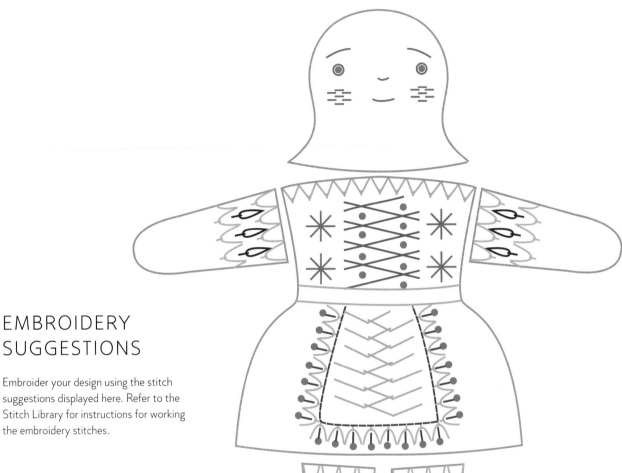

EMBROIDERY SUGGESTIONS

Embroider your design using the stitch suggestions displayed here. Refer to the Stitch Library for instructions for working the embroidery stitches.

- Back Stitch
- Herringbone Stitch
- Chain Stitch, Long-tailed Chain Stitch
- Detached Fly Stitch, Feather Stitch
- Satin Stitch, Star Stitch, Straight Stitch*
- French Knots

Note: I worked the doll's face using satin stitch for the eyes and mouth and small straight stitches of varying lengths for the nose and cheeks.

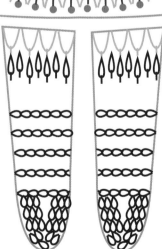

BOLSTER CUSHION

This little bolster cushion made from rich red upholstery linen and decorated with a sky blue felt braid, brings a touch of luxury to your home. The braid is cut using a scalloped template, and this is then embroidered before being stitched onto the linen fabric before the cushion is made up.

- -

YOU WILL NEED

One piece of red linen upholstery fabric 63cm x 51cm (25in x 20in)

Two pieces of blue felt 50cm x 8cm (21in x 3⅛in)

Stranded embroidery cotton (floss) in a choice of colours

Oddments of purple-red felt

2cm (¾in) wide pink cotton tape 60cm (24in) long for drawstring

Craft foam

41cm (16in) bolster cushion pad with a diameter of 15cm (6in)

MAKING UP

1. Machine zigzag around the edges of the red linen fabric to prevent fraying.

2. Trace the bolster braid template (see Templates) onto thin card and cut out. Use a pencil to draw around the card template onto the pieces of blue felt to create scalloped braids long enough to go around the circumference of the bolster. Cut out.

3. Embroider the felt braids using three strands of the embroidery thread (see Embroidery Suggestions).

4. Pin the finished braids to the fabric 12cm (4¾in) from each short end. Tack (baste) in place.

5. Sew a line of machine stitch between the top of the herringbone stitch and the buttonhole scallops (see Template) to attach the braids; remove the tacking (basting) stitches.

6. Now fold the fabric in half with right sides facing so that the long edges meet, and sew together with a 1.5cm (⅝in) seam allowance beginning and ending 9cm (3½in) from each end; press seams open.

7. To make the drawstring channel, at each end of the cushion, turn in and machine stitch a hem of 5cm (2in) leaving each end of the channel open for threading through the drawstring. Turn the cover right side out and insert the bolster cushion pad.

8. Use the button templates to cut out eight circles of felt and four of craft foam. Embroider each of the felt circles with a motif of your choosing (see Embroidery Suggestions).

9. Place a foam circle in between two felt circles and over-sew together. Make four buttons in all.

10. Cut the length of pink cotton tape in half and attach a button to one end. Thread the other end of the tape through the drawstring channel and then attach another button to the other end of the tape.

11. Pull the tape to draw it closed around the bolster end.

At a glance

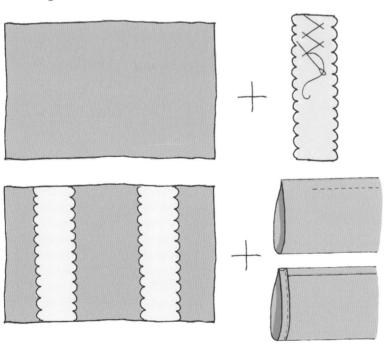

EMBROIDERY SUGGESTIONS

Embroider your design using the stitch suggestions displayed here. Refer to the Stitch Library for instructions for working the embroidery stitches.

● Herringbone Stitch

● Detached Chain Stitch

● Buttonhole Wheel Stitch

● Cross Stitch

---- Machine Back Stitch

Note: Repeat the braid embroidery design along the full length of the felt braid.

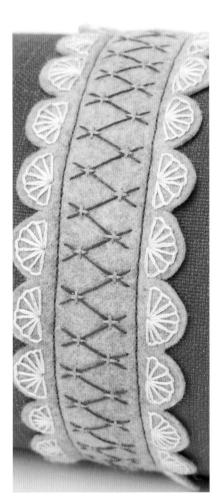

APPLIQUÉ PICTURES

Felt appliqué pictures are a great way to decorate your home. The flower picture is inspired by geometric 1960s designs and uses only the smallest scraps, making it ideal for leftovers. Just repeat the design as many times as you like to fit your frame. The folk-inspired bird picture offers a chance to practise a variety of stitches and it can be reduced or enlarged as you choose.

- -

YOU WILL NEED

White felt

Oddments of coloured felt

Stranded embroidery cotton (floss) in a choice of colours

Frame of your choosing

FLOWER PICTURE

MAKING UP

1. Cut the white felt to fit your chosen frame.

2. Trace the flower picture templates (see Templates) onto thin card and cut out the component parts.

3. Use a pencil to draw around the card templates onto your chosen felt colours and cut out your pieces.

4. Tack (baste) the flower circles and the triangle pieces onto your white felt background to hold them in place as you embroider.

5. Embroider the design using three strands of the embroidery thread (see Embroidery Suggestions).

6. Once your appliqué picture is complete, outline the flowers with running stitches.

7. Place the finished embroidery in your chosen frame.

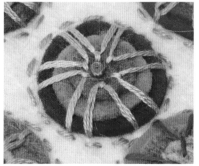

BIRD PICTURE

MAKING UP

1. Cut the white felt to fit your chosen picture frame.

2. Trace the bird picture templates (see Templates) onto thin card and cut out the component parts.

3. Use a pencil to draw around the card templates onto your chosen felt colours and cut out your pieces.

4. Tack (baste) the cut out felt pieces onto the white felt background to hold them in place as you embroider.

5. Embroider the design using three strands of the embroidery thread (see Embroidery Suggestions).

6. Once your appliqué is complete, outline the bird with running stitches.

7. Place the finished embroidery in your chosen frame.

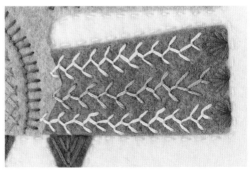
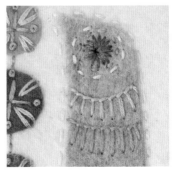
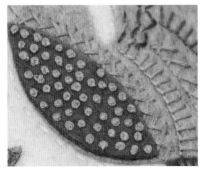

EMBROIDERY SUGGESTIONS

Embroider your designs using the stitch suggestions displayed here. Refer to the Stitch Library for instructions for working the embroidery stitches.

FLOWER PICTURE

- Running Stitch
- Detached Chain Stitch
- Fly Stitch, Detached Fly Stitch
- French Knots

BIRD PICTURE

- Running Stitch, Eskimo Laced Running Stitch, Whipped Running Stitch
- Herringbone Stitch
- Detached Chain Stitch
- Buttonhole Stitch
- Fly Stitch, Feather Stitch
- Double Star Stitch, Straight Stitch
- French Knots

Flower Picture

APPLIQUÉ PICTURES

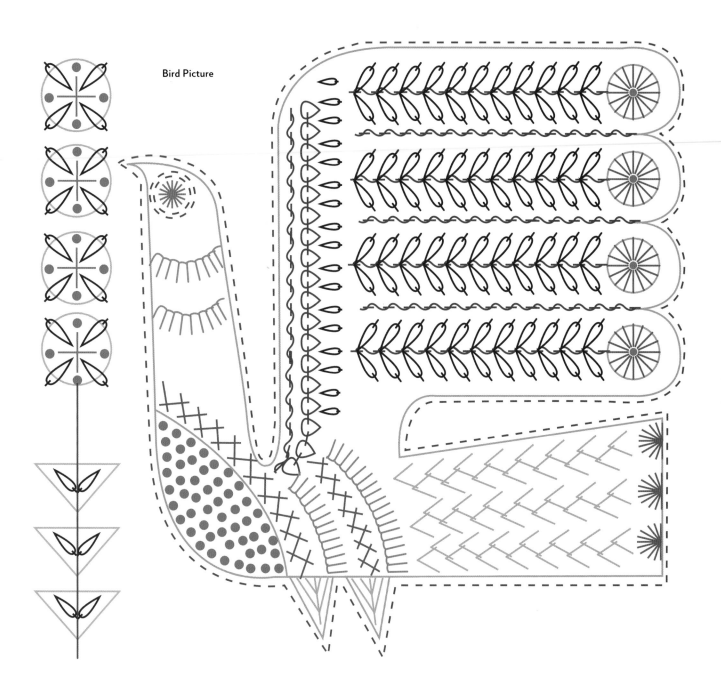

Bird Picture

CRAFT BAG

This is a really useful craft bag to keep all your materials in while you are on the move. It is made in heavyweight linen and embroidered in 2-ply tapestry wool (yarn) but you could use three strands of stranded embroidery cotton (floss) if you prefer. It has an easy drawstring closure with decorative button pulls.

YOU WILL NEED

One piece of heavyweight linen fabric 58cm x 30cm (23in x 12in)

One circle of heavyweight linen with a diameter of 20cm (8in)

Lining fabric 0.5m (½yd)

2cm (¾in) wide decorative cotton tape 60cm (24in) long for drawstring

2-ply tapestry wool (yarn) in a choice of colours

Oddments of felt

Craft foam

MAKING UP

1. Cut two pieces of the lining fabric to match the heavyweight linen fabric pieces, as well as two additional pieces measuring 6cm x 32cm (2½in x 12½in) for the drawstring casing.

2. Machine zigzag around the edges of the large rectangle of linen fabric to prevent fraying.

3. Use the iron-on transfer method to transfer the flower design motif onto the large piece of linen fabric (see Templates and Techniques): find the centre of the fabric and mark with a pin to mark the front and back of the bag; transfer the design so it is centred on each side of the craft bag.

4. Embroider the design (see Embroidery Suggestions).

5. To make the casing for the drawstring, press a 1.5cm (⅝in) folded hem all around the long and short edges of the small strips of lining fabric.

6. Tack (baste) the casings onto the front of the bag 3cm (1⅛in) from the top edge making sure the ends butt up to each other leaving space for the drawstring, and machine stitch in place leaving the ends open to thread with tape later.

7. With right sides facing, machine stitch the sides of the bag together using a 1.5cm (⅝in) seam allowance.

8. Pin and tack (baste) the linen circle to the base of the bag.

9. Machine stitch together easing as you go. Trim seams to 5mm (¼in) and turn the bag right side out.

10. Now machine stitch the lining pieces together in the same way, but do not turn right side out.

11. Fold and press a hem all around the top of the lining and the bag.

12. Place the lining inside the bag and tack (baste) in place at the top.

13. Use the button templates to cut out four circles of felt and two of craft foam. Embroider the felt circles with a motif of your choosing.

14. Place a foam circle in between two felt circles and over-sew together leaving a small opening a little larger than the width of the drawstring tape.

15. Thread one piece of tape through one casing and loop it around to thread it back through the other casing so that its ends are at the same side. Slip the ends into the button opening and stitch closed to finish.

16. Repeat with the other piece of tape to make the drawstring on the opposite side of the bag.

At a glance

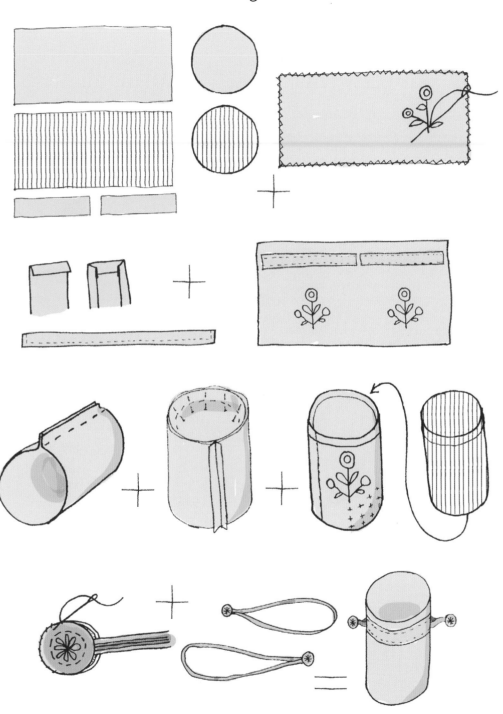

EMBROIDERY SUGGESTIONS

Embroider your design using the stitch suggestions displayed here. Refer to the Stitch Library for instructions for working the embroidery stitches.

- Running Stitch
- Chain Stitch
- Fly Stitch, Detached Fly Stitch
- Cross Stitch, Spider's Web Stitch

CRAFT BAG

SAMPLER PICTURES

These sampler pictures are a great way to practise a wide variety of stitches. Simply print off the patterns provided and transfer them to linen fabric and you are ready to go. The house sampler is particularly special to me as it was inspired by one made by my mother back when she was an art student after the war.

- -

YOU WILL NEED

Linen fabric in your choice of colour

Iron-on interfacing

Stranded embroidery cotton (floss) in a choice of colours

Frame of your choosing

HOUSE SAMPLER

MAKING UP

1. Cut the linen to fit your chosen frame and machine zigzag around the edges of the fabric to prevent fraying.

2. Iron interfacing onto the back of the linen – use a damp cloth to ensure the two layers are bonded thoroughly. The interfacing will stabilize the felt while you embroider.

3. Use the iron-on transfer method to transfer the house sampler design to the fabric (see Templates and Techniques).

4. Embroider the design using three strands of the embroidery thread (see Embroidery Suggestions).

5. Using a damp cloth again, press to finish and place in your chosen frame.

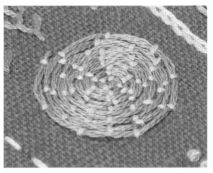
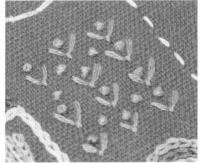

BUTTERFLY SAMPLER

MAKING UP

1. Cut the linen to fit your chosen frame and machine zigzag around the edges of the fabric to prevent fraying.

2. Iron interfacing onto the back of the linen – use a damp cloth to ensure the two layers are bonded thoroughly. The interfacing will stabilize the felt while you embroider.

3. Use the iron-on transfer method to transfer the butterfly sampler design to the fabric (see Templates and Techniques).

4. Embroider the design using three strands of the embroidery thread (see Embroidery Suggestions).

5. Using a damp cloth, press the finished embroidery. To complete the sampler with a fabric edging, see Techniques. Place the embroidery in your chosen frame.

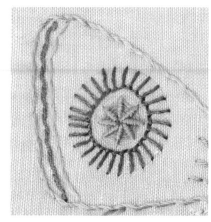
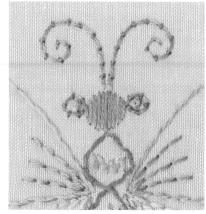
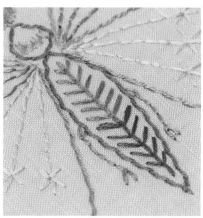
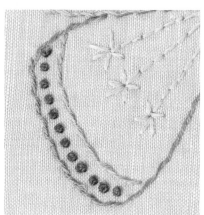

EMBROIDERY SUGGESTIONS

Embroider your design using the stitch suggestions displayed here. Refer to the Stitch Library for instructions for working the embroidery stitches.

HOUSE SAMPLER

- ● Couching, Running Stitch, Laced Running Stitch
- ● Chain Stitch
- ● Fly Stitch, Detached Fly Stitch, Feather Stitch
- ● Star Stitch
- ● French Knots

BUTTERFLY SAMPLER

- ● Couching, Whipped Running Stitch, Back Stitch*
- ● Herringbone Stitch
- ● Buttonhole Flower Stitch
- ● Fly Stitch, Detached Fly Stitch
- ● Satin Stitch, Spider's Web Stitch
- ● French Knots

*Note: I have used whipped running stitch to outline the butterfly's wings and body, back stitch for the legs and the lines radiating out from the body, and couching for the eye outlines and antennae.

TECHNIQUES

TRANSFERRING TEMPLATES

Here are three methods for transferring templates and patterns to fabric to provide you with guide lines for your embroidery stitches.

Card template method: Trace off the template onto thin card and use an air-erasable pen to draw around the design onto your fabric. The lines will gradually disappear without leaving a mark.

Iron-on transfer method: Print out the design onto paper and trace over the lines with an iron-on transfer pen. Lay the paper pattern side down onto the fabric and apply a hot iron until the line has been transferred: hold it in place firmly and intermittently check to make sure it is working well.

Window method: Print out or trace the design onto paper, and tape the paper to a sunny window. Tape the fabric in place on top of the paper and use an air-erasable pen to trace the design onto the fabric.

ADDING A FABRIC BORDER

I often back my embroidered pictures or samplers with felt or wool to pad them for added texture, and edging with a small print fabric border is a great way to finish the embroidery before setting it into your chosen frame.

1. Cut four 2cm (¾in) wide strips of your chosen fabric, two measuring the same length as the short sides of your embroidery and two measuring about 1cm (⅜in) longer then the long sides (to allow for turning in at the corners).

2. With the front of the embroidery facing you, align the shorter fabric strips to the short edges of your embroidery and machine sew in place using a 1cm (⅜in) seam allowance.

3. Fold and press a 1cm (⅜in) hem along the other edge of the fabric strip and turn it to the back of the embroidery to encase the raw fabric edge. Slip stitch in place.

4. Join the long fabric strips in the same way, this time turning in at the corners to encase the raw edges and hand sewing to finish.

COVERING A SELF-COVER BUTTON

To embellish your project with an embroidered button, all you will need is a self-cover button in a size of your choosing, a scrap of the project fabric, and a needle and thread.

1. Cut out a circle of fabric large enough to be gathered over to the centre of the self-cover button.

2. Sew gathering (running) stitches around the edge of the circle using doubled sewing thread.

3. Put the button in the middle of the fabric circle and draw up the thread to enclose it; fasten off the thread securely.

4. Put the button back over the shank and push firmly to snap shut.

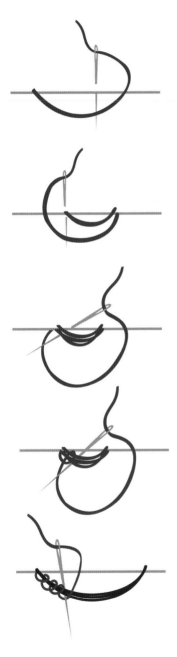

MAKING A BUTTONHOLE LOOP

It is very easy to work a buttonhole loop by hand to keep the lid of an embroidered pot closed.

1. Using all six strands of the embroidery thread in your needle, knot one end of the threads and lose the knot in the seam.

2. Create the foundation of your buttonhole loop by passing the thread three times back and forth (see diagram), ensuring that the size of the button you have chosen will pass through the loops.

3. Starting at one end of the loops, work buttonhole stitches closely together. Continue to the end to completely enclose the foundation threads.

TEMPLATES

The templates for the projects have been supplied full size.
Full sized templates can also be downloaded from the Stitch Craft
Create website at: http://ideas.stitchcraftcreate.co.uk/patterns/

CIRCLES CUSHION

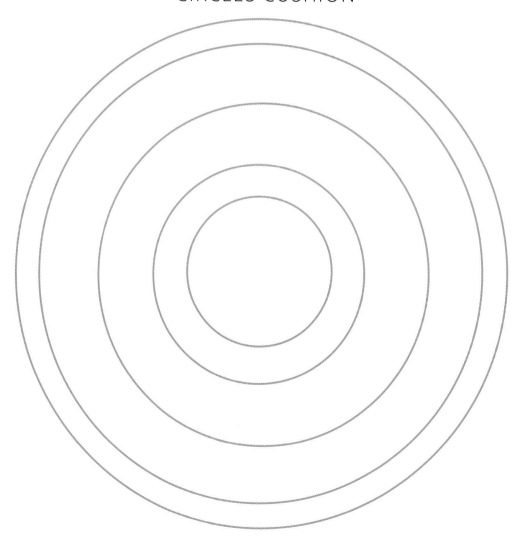

BROOCHES

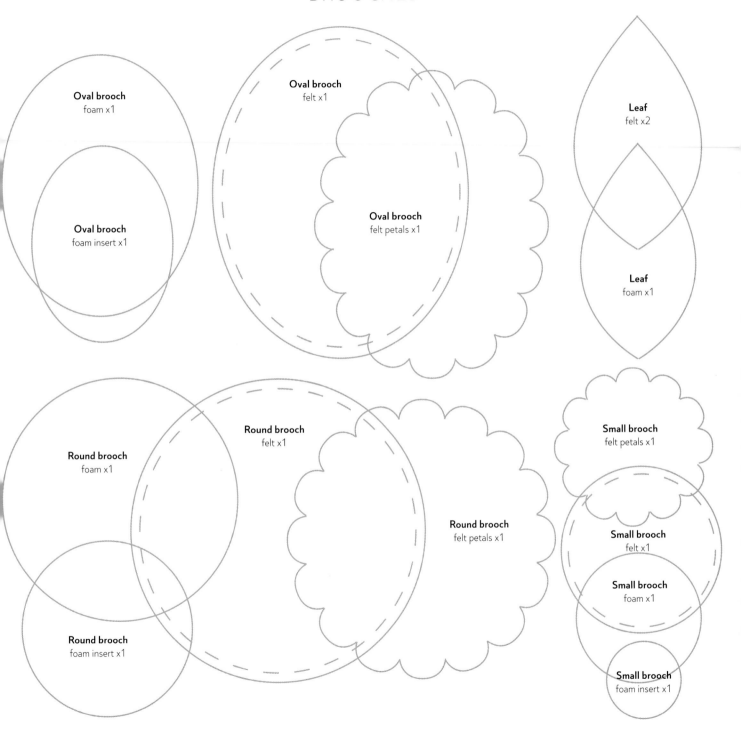

Oval brooch
foam x1

Oval brooch
foam insert x1

Oval brooch
felt x1

Oval brooch
felt petals x1

Leaf
felt x2

Leaf
foam x1

Round brooch
foam x1

Round brooch
felt x1

Round brooch
felt petals x1

Round brooch
foam insert x1

Small brooch
felt petals x1

Small brooch
felt x1

Small brooch
foam x1

Small brooch
foam insert x1

PINCUSHIONS

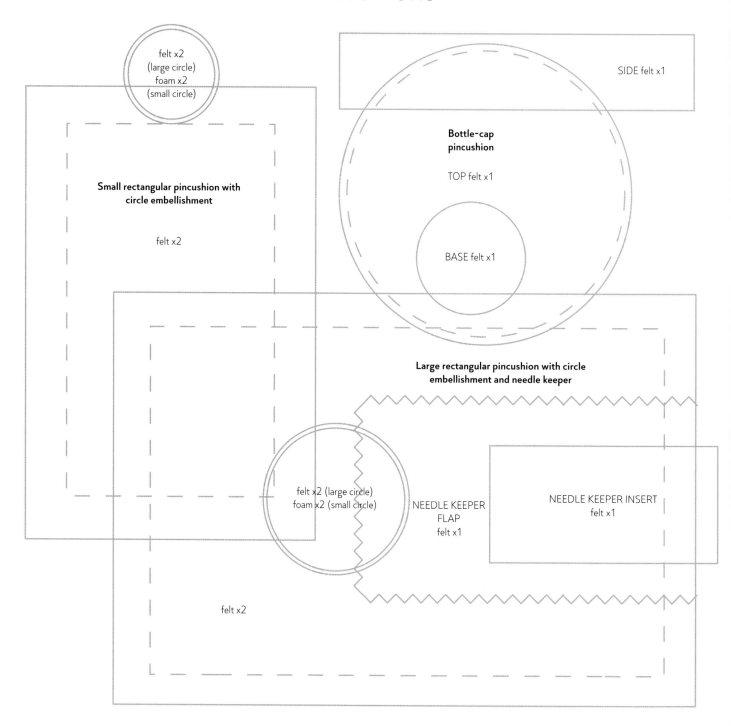

felt x2
(large circle)
foam x2
(small circle)

SIDE felt x1

Bottle-cap pincushion

TOP felt x1

Small rectangular pincushion with circle embellishment

felt x2

BASE felt x1

Large rectangular pincushion with circle embellishment and needle keeper

felt x2 (large circle)
foam x2 (small circle)

NEEDLE KEEPER
FLAP
felt x1

NEEDLE KEEPER INSERT
felt x1

felt x2

GEOMETRIC GARLAND

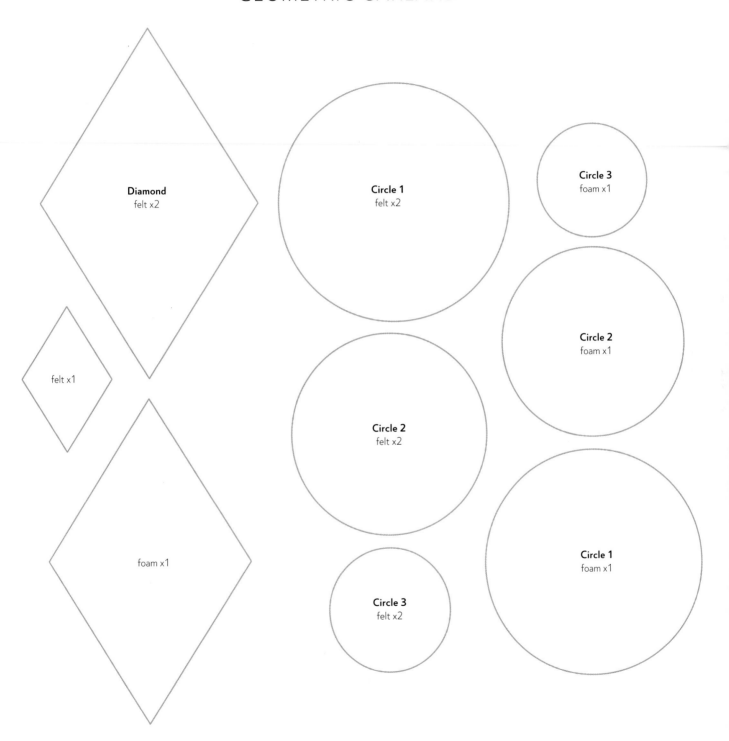

Diamond
felt x2

felt x1

foam x1

Circle 1
felt x2

Circle 2
felt x2

Circle 3
felt x2

Circle 3
foam x1

Circle 2
foam x1

Circle 1
foam x1

THREAD CATCHER

FLOWER PICTURE

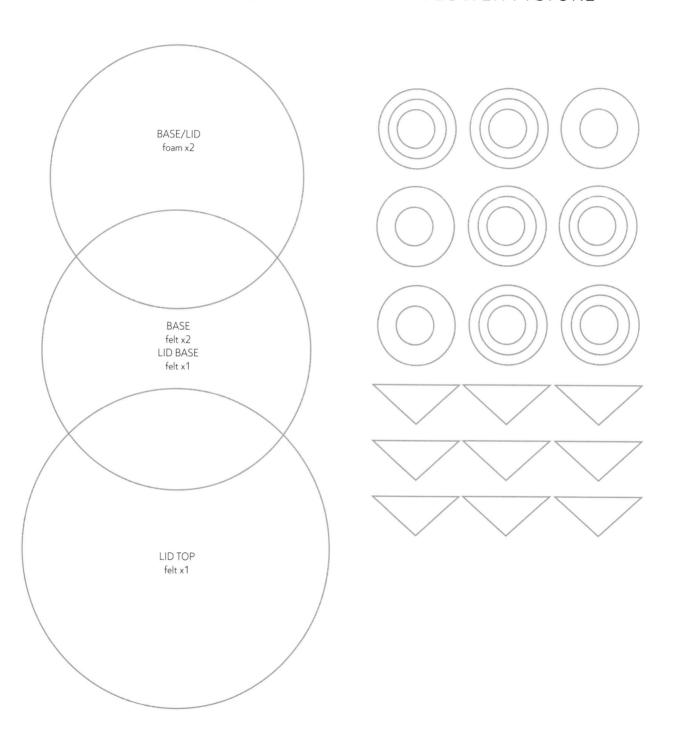

BASE/LID
foam x2

BASE
felt x2
LID BASE
felt x1

LID TOP
felt x1

TEMPLATES

BIRD PICTURE

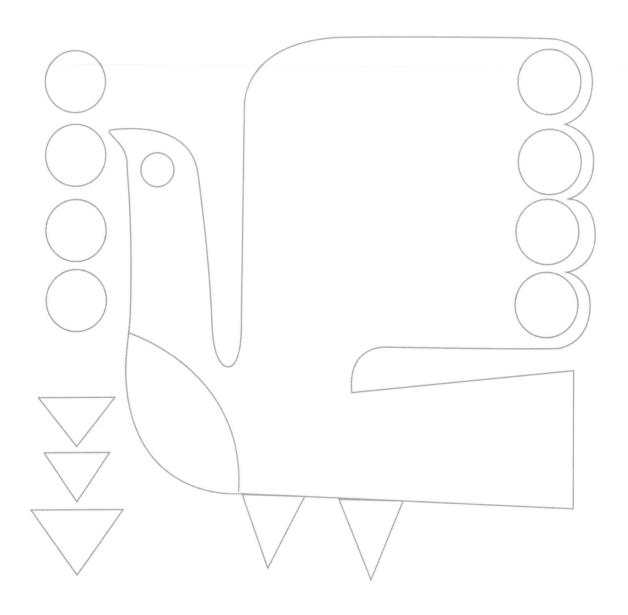

BOLSTER CUSHION

FOLK DOLL

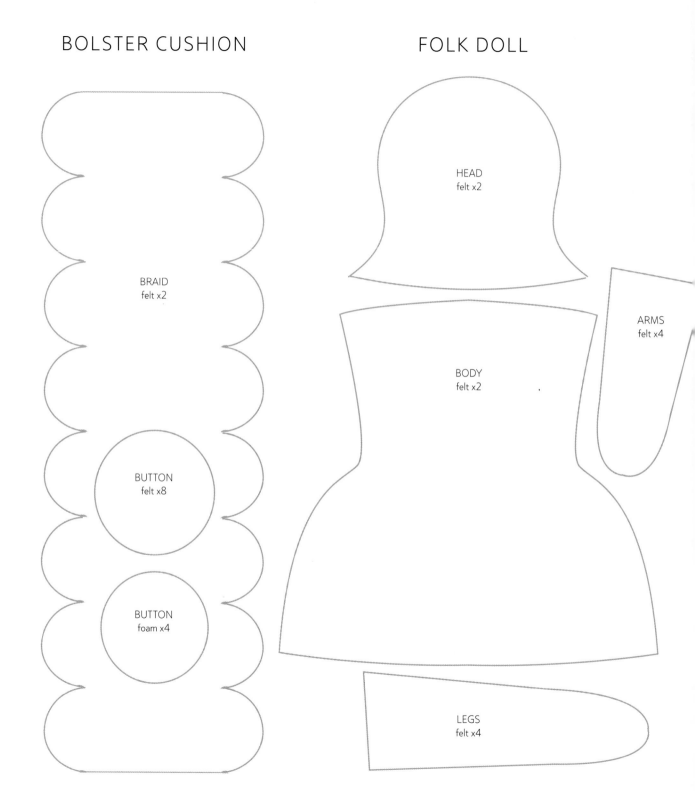

BRAID
felt x2

BUTTON
felt x8

BUTTON
foam x4

HEAD
felt x2

BODY
felt x2

ARMS
felt x4

LEGS
felt x4

CRAFT BAG

BUTTON
foam x2

BUTTON
felt x4

HOUSE SAMPLER

BUTTERFLY SAMPLER

ABOUT THE AUTHOR

Nancy Nicholson is a leading embroidery designer well known for her folk art inspired patterns and motifs. She has developed a unique and distinctive style for decorative embroidery which has a very modern aesthetic but is based on traditional techniques.

Nancy sells her designs and kits online and has a fast growing, loyal following of international fans. She has an impressive arts and crafts pedigree and is following in the footsteps of her mother, Joan Nicholson, an accomplished embroidery designer and author.

www.nancynicholson.co.uk

SUPPLIERS

FELT
www.cloudcraft.co.uk
www.paper-and-string.net
www.FuzzyFish.etsy.com

BOILED WOOL
www.etsy.com

CRAFT FOAM
www.hobbycraft.co.uk

FABRICS
www.clothhouse.com

THREADS
www.sewandso.co.uk

INDEX

I would like to dedicate this book to my mother who set me on this path, and to Tom and Will, my two boys who continue that path into their own very creative lives.

A DAVID & CHARLES BOOK
© F&W Media International, Ltd 2016

David & Charles is an imprint of F&W Media International, Ltd
Pynes Hill Court, Pynes Hill, Exeter, EX2 5AZ

F&W Media International, Ltd is a subsidiary of F+W Media, Inc
10151 Carver Road, Suite #200, Blue Ash, OH 45242, USA

Text and Designs © Nancy Nicholson 2016
Layout and Photography © F&W Media International, Ltd 2016

First published in the UK and USA in 2016

A catalogue record for this book is available from
the British Library.

ISBN-13: 978-1-4463-0629-1 paperback
ISBN-10: 1-4463-0629-1 paperback

ISBN-13: 978-1-4463-7465-8 PDF
ISBN-10: 1-4463-7465-3 PDF

ISBN-13: 978-1-4463-7466-5 EPUB
ISBN-10: 1-4463-7466-1 EPUB

Printed in China by RR Donnelley for:
F&W Media International, Ltd
Pynes Hill Court, Pynes Hill, Exeter, EX2 5AZ

10 9 8 7 6 5 4 3 2 1

Acquisitions Editor: Sarah Callard
Desk Editor: Michelle Patten
Project Editor: Cheryl Brown
Design Manager: Anna Wade
Editorial Assistant: Emma Fletcher
Production Manager: Beverley Richardson
Photography: Jason Jenkins
Design, Art Direction and Styling: Anna Wade

F+W Media publishes high quality books on a wide
range of subjects. For more great book ideas visit:
www.sewandso.co.uk

Layout of the digital edition of this book may vary
depending on reader hardware and display settings.